THE BOY NAMED BOBBIE

Bobbie Bell

Copyright

For permission requests, write to the publisher at the address Premium Book Publishers 15500 Voss Road, Suite 603, Sugar Land, TX 77498

Visit our website at www.premiumbookpublishers.com

First Edition: September, 2023

Book Published by Mr. Chris Walker & Mr. Bracken Joseph on behalf of Premium Book Publishers.

DEDICATION

This book is dedicated to God, the creator of all with love and gratitude. God was with me in the beginning. He then allowed me to learn and grow on my own. And God finally returned to guide me. Showing me unconditional love. Without you I am nothing.

Table of Contents

ACKNOWLEDGMENTS

Thank you to Premium Book Publishers for making this possible. Thank you to the team that made this book happen; Illustrator William Jacob, Formatter Ethan Parker, and Director Adam Benson. I express my grateful appreciation to Chris Walker and Bracken Joseph for their guidance, direction, and homework.

PREFACE

Growing up and living such an eventful life. I always said to myself, "I'm gonna start a journal and eventually write a book." I wanted to share my stories and wonderful experiences with everyone. Someone on the planet would enjoy my stories. Someone may even learn from my wins or my losses. I never started that journal. Thank God for giving us the ability to remember.

Even as a young child, I always said to myself, "I know there is more to this life." As a child I didn't understand how life worked, or was "Supposed to work". So I lived in my innocent mind with my thoughts.

Once I matured I thought back and realized God was always there. Believe me, these aren't just filler words to make someone feel better about themselves. God was always there for me. Therefore he's always there for you. You truly are not alone.

As a child I had experiences that I assumed were "Normal" because it was normal to me. For example as a child I began to see a blue dot. It would appear every once in a while just before I fell asleep. As it floated around doing figure eights etc… I would talk to it as if it were my best friend. It never responded verbally but I knew it understood me.

Throughout my lifetime I saw the blue dot. At one point I told a girlfriend about the blue dot. She appeared to believe me. She even asked me randomly if I was still seeing it. Which made me love her more at the time.

Other than her I told no one. If I did, I honestly don't remember doing so. In our culture in the US seeing a floating blue dot might get you locked up in the psych ward. Recently I came across a book titled, "From the Finite to the Infinite" featuring "Swami Muktananda". He described the blue dot as" the

Blue Pearl." Which gave him great joy and enlightenment. At that very moment I realized the blue dot/blue pearl was more meaningful than I had known.

You know how people say, you're not alone, you always have God, and God is always by your side? It is true, it is fact! I have seen and lived it. You are not alone, don't give up. God is factually present in your heart. Do your own research. The closer you get to him, the more you'll feel the power of his presence in and around you. May God bless you!

CHAPTER 1

CHICAGO

"Who am I, you sure you want to know? This story of my life is not for the faint of heart." A simple quote by Peter Parker in which I would guess most people on the planet could relate to. For me, it was right on.

My story begins in the year of 1971 in Chicago Illinois. The South side of Chicago in fact.

Picture this, as you leisurely stroll through the fluffy snow on the school yard. You see a child sitting in the upright fetal position. Head positioned downward between his legs using his winter jacket with a hood as a shield. As another child circles and uses the kid on the ground as a trampoline.

Yup, that was me on the ground. The tramp if you would. I was 5 or 6 years old. I don't remember all of the details. I do remember that earlier in the day the attacker attempted to bully me verbally. I refused to be bullied. I also refused to fight. Fight? I was no more than 6 years old and fighting was foreign to me. I did not understand the action of fighting. The thought of fighting or even arguing made me literally sick to my stomach.

Sometime later, my teacher called my mom to the school in order to discuss my changed/poor behavior. My mom and I met with my teacher at the school. I waited in the hallway as they entered the classroom. My mom exited the classroom a while later and appeared to be upset. My mom said with restraint in her voice, "No one calls my baby dumb!" When we arrived at the house my mom waited for Mitchell to get home. Mitchell was my step-father.

Once he arrived home they discussed the school incident. Apparently the teacher said my behavior was unsatisfactory. The teacher stated to my mom she thought I behaved as if I was mute. She said I wouldn't participate in any of the classroom activities. She said outright that I was "dumb". I figure that was when my mother had had enough. Janet pulled me from the school. By the way, I referred to my mom as Janet, not mom.

Little did they know I was getting stomped out every day by the school bullies, I didn't understand why they continued to beat me up. I did not want to be there. I didn't rat the kid out because I was afraid the beatings may have gotten worse. My mom saved me. As I write I'm having epiphanies and realizations. Janet, my beautiful mother in heaven. I forgive you.

Not only because you saved my life in that situation. But because I realize you tried your best. I never attended a school in Chicago again after my mother pulled me from that class.

CHAPTER 2

SELF DEFENSE MECHANISMS

In my case, I refused to accept the reality of what was happening. My denial blocked the event and the circumstances from my mind. I was avoiding the painful feelings that I had to deal with emotionally. I had no idea how to deal with my reality. And no one around me had the keys to the safe.

Let's go back to the first memories I had as a child. They were images of my mother and father lying naked in their bed. I woke up one morning before anyone in the apartment. I was a toddler and wanted to see my mom. Their bedroom door wasn't fully secured so I pushed the door open. I was startled to see my mother and father asleep, naked and sprawled on top of each other.

I remember them being grimy and sweaty looking. Once I began to understand what I was seeing. I realized they were still asleep. I then carefully backed out of the room and attempted to close the door. Once the door made a creaking sound, I immediately stopped closing it and went back to bed. Later that morning my father questioned my sisters and me. He asked who opened his bedroom door. My sisters said nothing, nor did I.

This memory was made in the infamous Cabrini Green Housing Project. I remember the filthy elevators, and the metal caging surrounding us as we walked through the projects. The metal caging is what secured you from falling multiple stories to your death. Not a brick and mortar exterior wall like other buildings. I felt like a mouse in a maze.

Another traumatizing memory I had that also occurred in the Cabrini Green Housing Project was of me climbing into our bathroom sink in order to take a bath. I remember thinking I was a big boy and could bathe myself. With my sister's assistance I climbed into the sink. The water was turned on and that was when things went south. I don't remember who turned on the water. Once it was on it flowed onto my upper thigh. It started off room temperature, then slowly became scorching hot. I was a toddler and must have been in shock. I didn't move even as my skin began to blister. I must have been screaming because my mom ran into the restroom and saved me. Needless to say, I have a birthmark and a reminder that the Cabrini Green Housing Project existed.

CHAPTER 3

KING

On a lighter note, let me tell you about the love of my life. His name was King and my sisters introduced him to me. I was outside having a blast by my lonesome and my sisters and I heard a puppy crying from a home across the street from our house. We approached the backyard fence where we heard the puppy crying.

Once our eyes met, it was love at first sight. He was a beautiful brown German shepherd puppy. Once he saw and sniffed us, it appeared to trigger the puppy. He cried and cried which plucked on all of my heart strings. With the influence of my sisters I got the puppy out of that evil prison and into my loving arms.

Later that day, our parents asked us where we found the puppy. Eventually the truth came out that we stole the dog from the neighbor across the street. I knew the dog didn't belong to us and taking him from the neighbor was in fact stealing. With my naivety and a bit of encouragement from my older sisters. I grabbed the pup and believed we were heroes for doing so. I believed we were saving the pup from the clutches of evil that lived in that home. If they left him outside, then surely he'd easily end up in a pot of stew. You know, like Hansel and Gretel. There was no doubt in my fragile mind that he had to be saved immediately.

Mitchell grabbed the puppy and escorted us kids across the street. The neighbors came outside and Mitchell asked us, "Do you kids have something to say?" We then said in unison we were sorry for stealing their dog. The neighbor basically said you're forgiven, but stop stealing! The neighbor also said that they noticed the dog was in love with me. He's imprinted on you said the gentleman of the home. We came to the agreement that he was my dog now and mine alone. I was responsible for feeding him and cleaning up his poop.

Mitchell said, "He stays outside!" Which kinda made me sad. Universal balance strikes again. I was with King every moment I could. We gave each other unconditional love. He was my best friend. The home we lived in had an attic, a basement, a front and back yard. Prince and I had some serious territory to cover within our future adventures. It tore me up at the end of day when we had to part ways. I made sure to tell King how much I loved him. I gave him hugs and let him know I'd see him in the morning.

Almost every morning I was up early so King and I could hangout. Another reason I woke up early was the Shy-Town sunrise. As a child I loved the morning sun and the perfect silence of the world. I felt a sense of peace and power in that moment. As if the sun gave me life. I was awestruck with its beauty. I obviously wasn't the same as the other kids from around the hood.

One day as King and I were playing in the backyard. I decided to play Spider-Man. So I went to the side walk in between our house and the neighbor. I would get a running start then jump onto our backyard fence. I would stick to it like Spider-Man sticking to a wall. After I tried it a few times I was a pro. So I used a marker and would pull it back after each jump to see how far I could jump. On the next jump that I executed, I noticed a small block of wood with three nails protruding from it. The size of it was approximately 6 to 8 inch 2x4. I looked around wondering where it came from. I was like, oh well. I moved the block out of the way and was on to the next jump. I vividly remember making sure the nails were pointed down. I then walked to the front yard to get a running start. I ran like the wind! Neither the Green Goblin nor Doctor Octopus were a match for my super speed. I jumped like a human spider. Apparently a human baby spider in training because I missed my mark. I landed on the ground and realized there was a nail protruding through my foot. It was the nail and wood block that I had moved a minute ago. I screamed and fell to the ground. My mom ran outside and saw the block attached to my foot. She immediately took me to the hospital with the block attached. In the end I healed properly and all was well.

CHAPTER 4

YOU NEED SOME HUMAN FRIENDS BOY

The question is…who placed the block with the nails up on my path? And it was done twice in fact. As a child I never thought twice that someone would target me with such a horrible act with malicious intent. Why would I?

Once I healed up, Mitchell decided to buy me some new clothes and take me on a trip to join the boy scouts. From what I could remember I was totally up for it. After all, they were like superheroes in training right?

Once we arrived at the park where they were in training and signing new recruits in. I was introduced to everyone. Everyone was super kind, but I immediately felt uncomfortable.

The vibe was off and the atmosphere felt a bit dark. Mitchell apparently saw the change in my facial expressions and body language. He then pulled me aside and asked what I thought about joining the scouts. I said no thank you. Mitchell didn't question me and took me home. Mitchell was a hero and did what heroes do. He saved the day.

I appreciate Mitchell attempting to toughen me up and introducing me to children my age. I was a super sensitive child. My sisters made me cry almost every day of my youthful life.

Honestly they didn't have to do much to make me cry either. The truth is I wasn't crying because I was physically soft. It was something else.

CHAPTER 5

SUBSTANCE ABUSE

Mitchell was a violent alcoholic. And my mom was an alcoholic and a substance abuser. A perfect recipe for disaster. It was a Saturday night with family and friends over. Everyone appeared to be happy as they drank, smoked and whatever else they were doing. There were people everywhere in our house. Complete strangers doing as they pleased. I actually had a good time until my mom and dad started fighting. Then the party was over.

The following week or so we had family over. My stepdad was power drinking and playing blues music. It was approximately 2pm at the time. My mom and dad began verbally fighting. Some family including my Granny was over at the time. Granny wasn't having it. Eventually everyone in the house was fighting verbally and it was getting physical. That was my que and right on point I started crying. I had so much anxiety and fear I didn't know what else to do. One of my female cousins picked me up and took me into another room. She laid me in the bed and hugged me until I stopped crying. I remember milking it. She made me feel like I mattered. That type of affection was something I wasn't accustomed to. I don't remember seeing anyone receive that type of love in our home. There was no consistent love, affection, hugging, or kissing. I saw it on Good Times and The Brady Bunch so I knew we were different.

A few days later in the evening some time. I was in my room playing with my imaginary friend. His name was Casper. Yes, Casper the friendly ghost. Every once in a while, Wendy the witch would hang out with us. As we were having a blast in my room, I heard my mom call for me. I arrived in the living room to see my mom lying on a gurney with paramedics restraining her.

Janet looked almost unrecognizable. I'd never seen her look like that. Her eyes were red, puffy and almost closed. Her speech was slurred. Her hair was all over the place. In a calm yet eerie voice Janet told me she loved me. She asked, "Do you love me?" I replied, "Yes." She said, "Then go get my medicine. You know where it is. Please get mommy's medicine." I remember thinking, oh, I'll go get it. Then I looked around and everyone was staring at me. It made me uncomfortable so I didn't move. I also had no clue where her medicine was. As the paramedics wheeled her out, she continued begging me to get her medicine.

Those unlucky paramedics. They heard the call on their radios and responded like the heroes they were. Little did they know they would probably need therapy after a minor call. After all the events I was able to suppress. This incident remains vividly in the corner of my mind.

I was told my mom took too many pills and had to go to the hospital to get better. Once she returned home, it was like nothing happened. There was no counseling, therapy, or explanations. Simply back to business as usual.

CHAPTER 6

KNUCKY

One evening at approximately 6pm. Mitchell was standing on the porch with some of our male neighbors. All of their kids and I were playing in the front yard. One of the kids was a Deebo level bully. An undiscovered Mike Tyson. His name was Knucky. That's correct, his name was Knucky. He had linebacker shoulders with no neck as a child. He was born powerful and aggressive.

Mitchell yelled and told me to come to where he was. I ran to the porch. He informed me that Knucky and I were going to fight. I thought, that's a good one, very funny. The fathers on the porch immediately began yelling at all the kids to get off the grass. At this point I was totally confused as to why the dads were clearing everyone off the grass. Then I noticed Knucky was the last one to get off the grass. And he wasn't budging. At that moment I realized what was going on. They were clearing the stage for my demise, my deletion, my murder! The 70's were no joke!

Mitchell demanded I get on the grass, so I did. Knucky then proceeded to put those knuckles on me. He pounded on a kid that had no clue how to fight, and didn't attempt to fight back. I had no reason to fight that future bruiser that was twice my size. I remember all the parents standing on the porch watching and laughing.

During the beating I was crying and literally begging my parents to stop baby Tyson from pummeling me. I was begging with my eyes. They didn't see me and I don't think they ever truly did. They were busy drinking, smoking and laughing to notice my internal pain. I was a joke to them, all the neighbors and their children. I was the weird kid on the block, the outcast. Unlike any of them.

Approximately a week later as we all slept. In my dreams I heard King barking. I didn't see him but I could hear him. It was an intense and continuous bark. I was then woken up by my mother and father. My mother explained that the garage (which was separated by the back yard) was on fire and King's barking woke them up which potentially saved our lives. The fire department was on site putting out the blaze. King was a hero, like Krypto the SuperDog! I always knew he had it in him. King was my best friend.

Days later my birth father called the house to say hello. He asked me the basic questions. How are you, how's the dog etc… One bit of information he gave me confused me for years to come. He informed me that he had remarried and had a new son with his new wife. That bit of information confused me for a second but I regained my composure and figured it out.

Wait, he had another bit of information. He informed me that his new son's name was Bobby Jr. That was when I became totally confused. It made no logical sense. You can't give him my name! There must be a rule against such Tomfoolery! This doesn't apply to George Foreman. They all live in the same home etc… You know what I mean.

I realized his new son's name was Bobby "Junior!" My name was just Bobby. It was like Bobby Jr. was his real son, and I was the imposter. I was born first! I wasn't jealous, I was disappointed. I immediately felt betrayed. I shut down and I stopped talking. Our conversation was over and that was the last time I ever heard his voice.

My father made choices, and I had none. Therefore his choices had nothing to do with me. I pray he is at peace with the choices he made. I feel no indignation, resentment, or anger towards my father. I hope he had a long and love filled life. I have no clue why he did what he did, and there is a reason for that. Either way, I love you and I forgive you father.

CHAPTER 7

GOD WAS PRESENT

I was five or six years old, playing in the front yard. A friend of the family named Floyd asked me if I wanted to go to the store. I said with an excited voice yes, yes I do. I assumed we were going to the store down the street with all the sweets. Nope, we ended up at Sears which was a bit further down the road. Once we arrived at Sears. Floyd directed me to slide all the jewelry into the bag he was holding. I was like, cool free stuff. When we returned home, it was after dark. My parents were furious! They let Floyd have it. Considering the fact he basically kidnapped me for a jewelry heist. I was fortunate to return home safe and sound. God was present.

Another incident that made me believe God was present. It was a Sunday and Mitchell took us fishing. It was a fun outing with the family. No major arguments, fights, or disagreements. My sister's friend Yolanda from down the block came along. She stepped on a hook and it got caught on her foot. I believe my sister pulled it out and Yolanda was good. Just like Ice Cube said, "Today was a good day".

Once we arrived home and pulled into our driveway. You could almost hear the record scratch and abruptly stop. All the neighbors down the block were standing outside their homes and staring at the police which were in the front yard of our next door neighbor's home.

So the story is one of the kids from our block was approached by a kid from another neighborhood. The kid wanted his bike. When the kid from our block refused, his rival shot him through the neck. The entire incident occurred in front of our home. The bullet went through his neck and entered the next door neighbor's living room window. Thus the police interviewing our next door neighbor. The one and only divine God was on our side, and kept us safe that day. I cannot confirm nor deny that the kid that died was Floyd. The kid that took me on a crime spree.

One day I decided I was going to play Spider-Man in the attic. I got a glimpse of the roof through one of our attic windows. Oh did my Spidey sense begin to tingle. I decided to do a bit of Spider-Walking outside on the roof. It appeared safe enough. I went out about three or four steps in Spider-Man style of course. After a minute or two I returned to my layer in the attic. Approximately 15 minutes later my mom burst into the room and yelled "were you out on the roof?!" "One of the neighbors came over and said you were out on the roof!" I couldn't deny it, my spidey sense failed me. Needless to say. I never spidey walked on the roof again. God was present.

CHAPTER 8

GOD'S GIFT

We never went to church or anything like that. My Grandmother did though. She went to the Kingdom Hall in Chicago. The Kingdom Hall was the Jehovah's Witness place of worship.

Being and serving as a Jehovah's Witness was an important part of her life. I wish I had spoken more to her about the religious, spiritual, and historical aspects of her life. I say this because she was so focused on her beliefs. She was brave and courageous. She was royalty walking around her neighborhood as if she was an average person. Believe me, she was "MOOR," and so am I.

She was a great human being. I physically heard her say the word damn twice in my life. And when the words exited her mouth you could see her cringe and grit her teeth. She tried her best for all of us. My Granny knew I wasn't like the other kids. I now realize she wasn't the same as the people that were around her either. She was brave enough to be different. Granny was my heart and I miss her dearly. My Granny (Christine Bates) was God's gift to the Earth.

I'm not sure what led to the next situation but this is what I remember. My Grandmother and an unknown man picked us kids up from our house. The stranger dropped us off in the middle of a Chicago winter snow storm. I remember us holding onto each other and walking, and walking. I didn't understand why we were walking in the snow when we could be back at home with King keeping me warm.

Once we arrived at our destination I thought finally we could be warm again. When we entered the home Granny then asked a man permission for us to stay there for the night. I remember the friend getting upset and not being sure they wanted us to stay at their home. Eventually they gave in and allowed us to not freeze to death. We were told to lay on the floor and be quiet. No pillows or blankets were provided. I was content to be inside and no longer walking in the wind and snow. Believe me, God is good.

A few days later we were all back home. I was a loner in my own home, so things were back to normal for me. As for the rest of the family. I did notice everyone was walking on eggshells. Not King and I, we were good.

Around this time Granny was making plans to move to Arizona. She was going to move in with her brother Howard. She planned for all of us kids to move with her to a town called Tucson. My Granny was an angel in a human vessel. My Granny and mother asked me if I wanted to move to Arizona with her and the girls. I wanted to go but who was going to take care of King? I also had to take care of my mom. King and my mom were worth the beatings I was receiving around the neighborhood.

So when it was time for them to depart, it didn't feel like a sad moment. I felt I would miss them but I was also happy to have the home to myself. Also the teasing and beatings would stop. Goodbye anxiety and hello blissful freedom.

I had a blast! King and I were loving life. Uninterrupted adventures at their best. No girls yelling, or harassing me. I wasn't their slave nor their punching bag anymore. I loved everything about my new found freedom.

Approximately a year later I was told I had to move to Tucson. I had no choice in the matter. All I could think about was King. I felt there was no way he could survive without me.

The Quality of life would most definitely change and not for the better. My heart was broken.

It was 'D' day and it was time to say goodbye to my King. I gave him as much love as humanly possible. I was told we were going to visit next year so I wasn't as sad as I could have been. I said my goodbyes to my friends on the block and then it was time to go.

Mitchell drove Janet and I to the bus station. Janet and I jumped on the Greyhound bus and sat in our seats. I looked up from playing with my super stretch Spider-Man doll and noticed Mitchell walking on the bus toward us. I thought it was peculiar. He then stood in front of us and said goodbye once again. He gave me a hug which was odd. I could smell stale alcohol through his pores. He then stood there staring at me. Then out of nowhere Mitchell punched me on the shoulder. The punch deadened my arm, and it really hurt. I was dumbfounded at that point. My mom told him to stop in a semi-aggressive voice.

I was wondering what I did to deserve to be punched like a man. I looked up at Mitchell with confusion. He stood there for a minute then exited the bus. From the exterior of the bus Mitchell placed his hand on the glass. I was confused once again. I turned and looked at my mom and thought, "Am I in the Twilight Zone?" Janet said put your hand on the window. I thought, no thank you, so I didn't.

Years later It came to me what Mitchell was doing. He punched me on the shoulder because he wanted me to cry. He desired a showing of emotion from me with the fact that we were leaving him. And the hand on the glass thing. Yup, he wanted me to place my hand on his hand as if it was a love story. It most definitely wasn't a love story. If it were, odds are the entire family would be in his home living our best lives.

The bus ride was awesome. I had a great time. I saw so many things I had never seen before. The downside of my first bus experience. I got sick on the bus. It was spontaneous. I tried to hold it in my mouth as my mom's eyes got huge. Then kaboom, all over the place.

There were even other passengers assisting with the clean-up. Another negative occurred when we changed buses. I forget my stretch Spider-Man on the last bus. He was gone forever. That one hurt me deeply.

CHAPTER 9

ARIZONA

I remember arriving in Tucson, Arizona. Everything seemed so bright. I noticed all the cactus and dirt. My Granny's brother and my great uncle Pete drove up to pick us up. My first impression of him was that he was a big and powerful man. He was wholesome and old school. A modest, tough guy. He was direct, honest and kind enough to allow 4 people to live in his home with his own family of 3. I thought my Uncle's house was nice as well.

My Uncle and two of his children were living in his home at the time, Hanky and Marcus. Marcus was closer to my age so we hung out. They had 3 dogs. I was quite happy for that. But of course it wasn't the same. Marcus was actually quite intelligent. When we played board games or cards, he mostly won. It was rubbed in your face for the rest of the evening as well. This is one of the reasons I didn't play board games or cards as much.

I wanted to have fun, not yell and scream at each other. Win or lose being a good sport was what I was all about. If I had to watch out for my family cheating in a card game, I'd prefer to sit on the bench.

Hanky, the eldest son was my hero. He was strong, fast, super melanated complexion and handsome. He got all the ladies which was probably due to him having such a kind soul. I loved him so much. We would have random Ramen noodle eating contest. For example, I'd be sitting on the sofa watching cartoons. He would burst through the front door and yell Geno, you ready?! (*Geno is my nickname*)

I would jump up and follow him to the kitchen. He would cook a single bowl of Ramen Noodles then hand me a fork. With the superhot noodles on our forks we would see who could eat the ramen with the least blows to cool off the steaming hot noodles. He won 100% of the time. I didn't care about losing, it was him sharing a piece of his life and time with me. Believe me it was a priceless act.

Marcus and I would watch Saturday morning cartoons together. Marcus was on point. No alarm clock, the kid was sharp. I asked him to wake me up when he woke up. Some days the cartoons would begin at 4:30am. I honestly tried but I couldn't do it. I realized the cartoons I missed were gone until the following Saturday. No internet at the time. It was the 70's when we had 4 or 5 channels and no such thing as DVR. There were VCR's but we couldn't afford one of those. So, I would then ask him to wake me up when the Superfriends came on. I miss my cousins dearly.

Marcus eventually got married and had a couple children. Hanky had a rough one. We lived in an era where/when cocaine and Marijuana were recreational drugs. Crack was introduced and no one read the fine print. The fine print for crack read. Once you try this, you won't be able to stop. Say for example crack was a computer download. Once it is downloaded into the most complex computer ever created to date. Which is the human brain. The download becomes one with your computer/brain. A permanent download with no exceptions. The only way to destroy the download would be to destroy the computer.

Crack, Meth, Fentanyl, Opiates, prescription pills…life destroyers.

Hanky was an addict and got into a bit of trouble. He was incarcerated for a few years. Once he was released he did well on the outside. One night he did some drugs and lit himself on fire. My hero was no more. I pray that God gives Hanky another chance on earth as a human. I have faith that he will because he had such a beautiful soul. I'm sure almost everyone that knew him would concur. Hanky, Marcus I love you guys with all my heart. It was a pleasure meeting and spending time with you gentlemen.

CHAPTER 10

BACK TO SCHOOL

The one thought I totally dreaded was I would have to go back to school. I didn't want to do it. I felt different about Arizona though. Everything seemed so much brighter. I hoped and believed the kids in the Arizona schools would be brighter individuals as well. I was always down for an adventure. This go round I had no choice.

I started in the 2nd grade. It wasn't bad at all. I actually enjoyed participating in all the activities. All of my fellow students were pleasant and considerate. Believe it or not there was hope that I may find a friend yet.

At recess the students from my class were in the school yard having a great time. Some kids were playing basketball. While others were on the monkey bars or kicking the soccer ball around chasing each other. Our teacher blew her whistle letting us know recess time was over. We would then run and form a line to enter the classroom. I turned and took two steps then bam! I hit something that felt like a brick wall. I then hit the ground and did what I did best, I started crying.

With tears in my eyes, I looked up and saw a giant figure. He then literally picked me up and immediately said, "I'm so sorry, are you ok?" He helped me brush myself off and said he was sorry like 10 times. The kid practically blocked out the sun and he was being kind when I was in distress. I was so confused I had no choice but to stop crying. If that scenario occurred in Shy Town, the kid would have open-hand slapped me while I was on the ground just to give me a real reason to cry. That kind giant eventually became a star football player at the University of Arizona.

After living with my great uncle for a year. My Granny borrowed money from my uncle in order to obtain an apartment for us. Low income housing of course. A blessing is a blessing and we were extremely grateful. Thank you uncle, you assisted us in greater ways than any of us knew at the time.

We moved onto a low income apartment complex called "The Menlo Park Apartments". My Granny didn't work so she qualified for food stamps and Federal assistance. As a child I believed that was how life worked. You get food stamps, you buy food. You get Federal assistance, you get school clothes. Believe me, I was content, happy, and had all I needed. I was truly blessed.

The apartment was pretty cool. It was cool because I had my own room. The two girls had to share. It appeared they were adjusting to the apartment just fine. And as for myself, Menlo Park was basically 20 steps away from our apartment. I had an entire park to work with. Needless to say, I was quite content. We were scheduled to start school in a few days. And us kids were ready thanks to my Alchemist Granny. That Kinda sounds like an anime superhero's name.

I started the third grade with optimism. I wore my checkered pants and matching button up shirt. Of course I topped it off with my favorite church shoes. Let me rephrase. Kingdom Hall shoes. I was all smiles on my first day of school, and it was a good one.

Our school was across the soccer field next to the playground. So Granny didn't have to pick us up after school. We could walk by ourselves and take the necessary playground swing pit stop when given permission from big sis. On occasion I would walk by myself.

One day as I walked home by myself. I walked past the playground, then past the soccer field. Carrying my violin and my book bag. I heard a feminine voice coming from the parking lot say hey, hey, hey. I looked over and I saw a man and a woman in the parking lot. The man was sitting in the driver seat of a car. The woman was standing on the passenger side with one foot in the car and one foot on the ground.

The woman yelled. "Do you want the rest of these french-fries? We're done eating, we're full."

The year was 1978 and there wasn't a whole lot of information distributed or televised in relation to kidnapping or human trafficking. When I looked over at those people, red flags were poppin like fireworks.

So once I looked over at the lady, I immediately shook my head no and began to walk faster. When I finally reached for the doorknob of our apartment. I looked back at the parking lot. The couple was already gone. I thought, yup they were trying to get me. I decided not to tell my Granny what happened because I didn't want to upset her. That was obviously a bad decision. Fortunately with God's assistance I never saw that couple again.

CHAPTER 11

SOCCER/FUTBOL

One day after school I went outside to see what I could discover. I noticed a few of my friends from school playing soccer on the field just outside our apartment. Eddie Cordova came over to me and asked if I wanted to play. I accepted his offer. The coach, Jesus 'Bebo' Lopez gave me the green light to play. That was the beginning of my soccer career. I had no clue what I was doing but I had a great time. After practice was over Bebo informed me that I couldn't play until next season. But if I wanted to practice I would have to get my parents' permission. I was so happy. I couldn't wait to get home and ask Granny for permission.

When I got home I ran to my Granny's room to tell her the great news. When I asked her she wasn't quite as excited as I was. Actually she didn't break a smile. She simply said she would think about it. Remember, my Granny was a devout JW. She had to make sure she remained within the guidelines of the JW rules.

A couple of days later my request was approved. The rules were that I could play. But if there was a JW event, it took precedence over soccer. Believe me, there will be many tears shed due to me not being able to play soccer.

Finally after practicing two days a week for half a season. The next season started and I will officially be on my first soccer team. It was such a glorious moment for me in my life. I had been through a lot in my 8 years of life on earth. Now it was my time to shine. And shine I did.

The coaches, team parents and my teammates were impressed with my performance in practice and particularly in games. I was a goal scoring machine. There were 4 or 5 kids on our team that stood out. We had a blast out there on the field. And the parents took great care of us.

There was one issue I still had that continued to haunt me on the field and off. Almost every time I fell to the ground or was bumped hard. I would remain in that position crying as if it was the end of the world. I remember the parents attempting to console and/or redirect my crying to no avail. They didn't quite have the formula to solve that problem. At least not at that moment.

At the last game of the season all of the coaches and parents gathered around us players and gave speeches. The head coaches, Fred and Gilbert, announced that there were 4 MVP players as opposed to 1. Eddie and I were among the 4. I wasn't expecting that. I was out there having fun and received an award. Now that was awesome! At that moment I realized you must work hard for yourself and your neighbors. If good things follow, it's all God's blessing.

Granny wasn't there for the presentation, nor were my sisters. Granny didn't attend any of my soccer matches due to her religious beliefs. And as for my sisters, I'm not exactly sure why they never walked 30 feet outside to watch me play. I'm not judging my sisters, but they apparently didn't care enough to show up. A few months later the next season began.

Yes I was still crying every time I fell to the ground. I was 10 years old at the time. One of my friends/teammates' mother noticed my issues on and off the field. She then took it upon herself to figure out and battle my Kryptonite. Not her Kryptonite, but mine. Believe me I realize now how blessed I was.

We were about to start an important match against a quality team. Christina Yebra approached me and said, "You are possibly the best player out there on the field. The problem is you cry every time you fall. You don't have to cry, and you don't have to fall and stay on the ground. If someone makes you fall, it's not personal. You fall and then you get back up to your feet. You show them what you're made of. Be strong Bobbie, you can do it. I know you can." Christina then said, "If you stay on your feet and not cry today, I will take the team to Chuck-E-Cheese!" It was on me now to save the day, no pressure.

The criticism and positive reinforcement provided by Christina was something I had only seen on tv shows like "The Brady Bunch" or "Different Strokes". My Granny tried her best with the knowledge she had. I thank you Granny and I love you for what you gave me mentally. What Christina did to assist me in discovering my mental strength ignited a complete transformation within me.

After the game I was nervous because I fell a couple times due to being knocked down. I popped back up and continued playing though. I slid a time or two but it was a part of the game. At times I misunderstood people because of my perspective. So I was hoping I properly executed what she was asking of me.

Christina approached me after the game and said I saw you fall a few times. And the one time you fell you scored a goal. She said she knew I could do it. Now keep it up. Let's go play some video games. Us kids jumped in the back of Bebo's truck and headed to Chuck-E-Cheese!

Approximately 5 years later, Christina passed on due to complications caused by cancer. Christina taught me so much and took great care of me. She was a gift to the earth, an angel. I will love her and the Yebra family forever.

It was now tournament time and we would be traveling to Phoenix for our games that weekend. My Granny knew the tournament was coming up and had already given me permission to go. Coach Richard advised us players we would need to give him a small picture and our birth certificates. Which will be used for tournament registration. My Granny found a picture but couldn't find my birth certificate. Granny searched everything and everywhere but couldn't find it. No birth certificate meant I would be ineligible to play.

Coach Richard asked Granny if we could obtain a new notarized original copy of the birth certificate from Chicago. Granny said yes. My Grandmother called my mom and Mitchell and asked them if they could get a birth certificate and mail it to Tucson. They said they would make it happen. My mom said it would take a week or so.

Saturday came and there was no birth certificate. It broke my little heart. Not playing Saturday wasn't all that bad. But Sunday at the Kingdom Hall was torture. The Kingdom Hall itself was fine. It was controlling my negative thoughts. Actually it was the lack of control. The entire time I was pretending it didn't bother me.

The birth certificate arrived just in time making me eligible for the final weekend of tournament matches. Patience was being taught to me early in my life. Trials and tests of patience in an honest pursuit of life will never cease. All we can do is prepare ourselves as much as possible and wait with patience. And to try our best to stay focused with God as our guide. You can't go wrong.

Summer in Arizona was no joke. So Granny set up a road trip back to Chicago for our Tucson family. I couldn't wait to see my King! All I remember thinking about was, "Will he remember me?" "I hope he remembers me." After a three day Greyhound bus trip, we were finally in Chicago. Once we arrived at the house. I asked for permission to go see my King.

Of course they said yes.

CHAPTER 12

THAT BOY CHANGED

I remember that moment vividly. It was dark outside. At approximately 8 pm I walked down the sidewalk to the back yard. Prince was an Alpha dog and didn't play around with his territory. So I felt the need for caution. He had been in plenty of fights with the dogs from around the hood. He had an undefeated record. So I walked to the backyard at a normal pace and tried to keep my excitement under control. When I arrived at the gate, my King was already there standing strong.

I talked to him like I did in the past. I watched him closely to determine if he remembered me. He looked at me as if I looked familiar but he wasn't wagging his tail. I put my hand close to the fence so he could smell me. His tail began to wag and I then entered the gate.

King recognized me but he didn't give me love the way he used to. It felt like he was disappointed that I left him or he simply hated it there. Either way it broke my heart.

The next morning King was all over me and it felt like old times. I was so grateful Granny took me to King. We spent all day together. We were in paradise on earth. Ignorance is bliss.

A few days later, Travis, who was Yolanda's younger brother and my "best friend". We were hanging out in front of my house. And just like old times he started harassing, poking, and bullying me. A few years ago his actions were an everyday event. It was the norm for us. He didn't realize it, but things were different now.

Once he started in on me I told him to stop. I was still quiet and reserved so I'm sure he assumed I'd be the old punching bag. Travis began to physically push me and say, "Are you mad, are you going to cry?" At that moment I sprung towards Travis like a panther. I remember seeing his wide eyes as he stumbled backwards.

He never saw it coming. No one saw that coming, not even myself. As Travis fell to the ground I pounced on top of him. Once I was on top of him about to ground and pound Mitchell grabbed me and pulled me off of him. At that point I didn't realize anyone was outside watching. Nor did I look for someone to save me. Apparently my focus sharpened while I was in little old Tucson.

I immediately started to rage-cry like Goku. But more like Ralphy in The Christmas Story. Mitchell said, "Wow, you were about to pummel Travis. I didn't know you had it in you." When people truly care and dedicate quality time towards one another. Their self-worth, courage, and spirit grows. I believe that's what happened in Tucson. My Granny, coaches, team parents, teammates, teachers and classmates all gave me strength.

When people say, thank God for the little things this is what they meant. The things that we can't physically touch, or don't quite see, understand or consciously think about but are in motion within our lives.

Those people gave me life. God is in all of us and they were all God. The little things that weren't so little.

The following day I went to Travis's house. I wanted to apologize for my actions. We talked for a few minutes. Travis basically said due to the fact that I cried and he didn't, he won the fight by default. I thought, nope, I won. But I told him ok that's fine. I was still a kid and as much of a puppet as Pinocchio was. I was content in knowing I had just discovered a new Super power.

On our last day in Chicago we said our goodbyes. I told King we would hang out again, and that I would see him again. I let him know I loved him more than anything on the planet.

Physically I never saw him again. My sisters told me that Mitchell got drunk one day and kicked him down the stairs. King ran away and never went back. I didn't really believe what my sisters told me but it didn't matter. I never saw my best friend again. My heart was broken.

We drove back to Tucson with a family friend in his station wagon. That was very kind of him. I think back about the fact that Granny, my mother and step father didn't have enough money all together to afford 4 Greyhound bus tickets. Granny and us kids were on welfare. I didn't know the financial status of my mother and stepfather. Maybe they were trying to save money. I get it and it appears times were hard back then. God bless them all. Either way the friend of the family got us home safe and sound.

Now I'm 11 years old, in the 6th grade and playing soccer for the 10 and 11 year old club team. The name of the team was Aztecas. School was fine. I did what needed to be done. I loved visiting with my friends at school, but I honestly didn't enjoy attending school. I'm sure half the school felt the same as I did. As for soccer, I loved it and my level of play was increasing rapidly.

Every day after school I would go outside and kick the ball against the wall separating the field from the apartments. I would practice new moves, juggling, and ball control. I also practiced my left foot more than my right foot. I wanted my left foot to have as much control as my right did. It worked.

Usually a random kid would show up and want to kick the ball around or Eddie would join me. I had another good friend that lived in the apartments that hung out with me. The kids name was Little Roy. So this was in the late 70's and he was the first lil I ever heard of. The second was Little Joe Y La Familia, and the third was Lil Rob. I grew up in a primarily latin neighborhood. And proud of it. Without them, there is no me.

Little Roy was a fantastic soccer player and an even better human. His family loved me and I loved them. I slept over at Roy's apartment every once in a while. They took care of me as if I was Roy's brother and their son. Thank you Santos family. You were and still are my sunshine.

It was tournament time and Coach Richard asked for our credentials once again. And once again my birth certificate was nowhere to be found. The Tournament was scheduled to start in a few days. I was a little ball of stress.

I figured I wasn't going to play in the tournament considering it took A week or so when Mitchell mailed it the first time. Mitchell made it happen though. He mailed it through Western Union this time. Western Union was on point with their deliveries.

I observed everyone scrambling and hustling to get my birth certificate sent in time for the tournament. Mitchell had to go downtown Chicago to get a copy of my birth certificate.

That had to have been a bit of a hassle. My coach paid for western Union and I assume he had to collect it from there as well. My Granny was the middle woman making telephone calls back and forth. Every call to Chicago was an extra charge to her bill.

I was very appreciative of everyone's effort to help me. It was a great feeling to be thought of and to feel important. I thought, "I must succeed, there is no other alternative." My output of effort, and my level of play rose immediately and exponentially. Mind over matter is a real thing.

Around the neighborhood I was the protector of my friends. This started after my visit to Chicago. Whenever my friends would get beaten up or bullied. They would ask me to walk them to school, or hang out with them in vulnerable situations. It actually worked for the most part. We were rarely approached by bullies when we were together.

By the age of 12, I had been in more fights than some have had their entire lives. At that time and many years after I was proud of my undefeated record. Now I believe if I had proper guidance. My fight record would be 0 for 0. Real and true strength is possessing the knowledge and the will power to choose not to fight. Which was a lesson I was not taught as a child.

CHAPTER 13

SCHOOL?

Jr. High school or should I say middle school was an awkward phase for me. My voice literally changed in the middle of a Choir solo tryout. I had hair growing in places I wasn't prepared for. As I walked from class to class, I remember crying for no apparent reason. I was always ashy and I couldn't afford Chap-stick. For me, Jr. High was awkward indeed.

Eddie and I spent most of our Jr. High lives in the boy's restroom. While students were in class, we were in the restroom shooting spitballs at each other. We would pretend to use the toilet whenever anyone entered the restroom. Needless to say my grades were horrible.

Therefore, I was ineligible to play soccer throughout my middle school life. I wasn't proud of my poor grades, but I do remember hating being in classrooms.

At home, Granny did her best. When my grades began going downward. I didn't possess anything of worth for her to take or restrict in order to persuade a change in my study habits. Honestly if she took soccer from me, negative things may have occurred. I did well enough to make it to high school. I was quite thankful for that.

As a child, when Granny took us shopping I could sense her stressing out. I would watch the vein grow on her forehead and listen to her quiet groans and moans. I would tell her I didn't want or need certain things. Food or clothing, it didn't matter. I would try my best to help my Granny to feel better. A lot of the times when we shopped I would tell Granny I will get certain things later. That was so that my sisters could get what they wanted. I could literally see the stress leave her body. We made it work.

My Granny couldn't afford cleats. I was given hand-me-down cleats from my fellow players. I was grateful for their kindness. Coach Thomas Ettrick bought me my first pair of brand new soccer cleats. Thomas and his son Orlando took me to a soccer store and bought me some awesome white cleats. I was and am grateful. Beautiful men with a beautiful family. Thomas and his beautiful daughter Zorida passed on. I love them all with all my heart and soul.

Bebo bought me my second brand new pair of awesome white cleats. Bebo and his wife Silvia took such great care of me. If I ever needed anything, they would have provided. There is no doubt in my mind. This also goes for

Eddie's mom Edilia. Another beautiful woman with a beautiful family. I'm not leaving anyone out because you are all in my heart. I love you.

I made it to high school. I couldn't believe it, but I did just enough. I was a 15 year old playing Varsity soccer. At the time I was just playing soccer. I didn't see it as an achievement. I did notice people around campus being extra nice to me. I assumed that was normal life in high school. Throughout the years I realized it was a blessing from my senior soccer mates.

Obviously I was still a virgin. Throughout the years I had a few super innocent relationships. Second base was my baseline. If a girl wanted to go further than that, she had to get with another kid. Because this kid doesn't have a clue. Sex wasn't on my mind. No girls were allowed to enter our apartment anyway.

Cursing wasn't allowed either. At least not in my Granny's presence. I can honestly say my Granny never heard a curse word exit my mouth. I'm quite happy about that. Outside the home and out of my Granny's presence was another story. My freshman soccer season I played quite well. At the end of the season we had an award ceremony. I couldn't make it to the award presentation. I was playing with the US Olympic development team. Later I was given the award for most improved player for the high school team. It was an honor. And as for the ODP team. I made the team, but I couldn't afford travel expenses. My dream of playing for the US Olympic team was cut short.

That summer I gave my virginity to a lovely girl from Menlo. Her name was Linda. I had no clue what to do. Thank God she was a kind and caring young lady. So it was over before I knew it. Sex is sacred. It is truly a gift from God. I was fortunate to have shared myself with such a beautiful soul.

That summer I also began playing soccer in the Menlo park Men's league. I had to get Bebo's and Granny's approval. Playing in the men's league was a game changer. My game simply got better and better. I was fearless and on fire.

School started and I was now a sophomore. Soccer was great. We had a few players from my club team and a few from opposing club teams. We had a solid team.

Early in the season we were playing a tough team with tough players. Our coach's first job was as a woodshop teacher. His second was High school soccer coach. Without him sacrificing his time we wouldn't have had a soccer team. Thank you coach. The experienced players assisted Coach whenever he needed a hand.

We were losing at half time. We were approximately 2 goals down. We were optimistic that we would come back and win. During the team talk Coach advised us that he was going to play the players that haven't played in a while. He took out four of five starting players and replaced them with players that haven't played either that day or a few games prior. The match ended in a loss for us.

The next day the same four or five players quit the team, myself included. We understood that the coach wanted everyone to play. But we were playing to win games. Due to our differences we decided to remove ourselves from the team. I have no regrets quitting that team. It wasn't for me.

It's now my junior year in high school and we were on our way to the first match of the season. The school bus dropped us off at our opponent's school. We exited the bus and began preparing for the game. As I was about to take my sweats off, the coach pulled me aside and advised me I was not eligible to play. I thought you had to know I wasn't eligible before I got on that bus. Actually I should have known as well.

I also realized I did that to myself. I didn't make the grades. Therefore allowing someone to control my fate. Which was why I was so disappointed but not upset with the faculty for their revenge strategy. If it was revenge, or if it was karma. It was most definitely a lesson.

It was a lesson, but my attitude never changed. The following year, which was my senior year, was a blur. Basically the same as last year. With the addition of drinking alcohol and going to parties. It was all about fun and no work. I had a great time. Sounds pretty awesome until you realize your GPA was garbage. I possessed professional soccer abilities and it was my senior year. I wasn't very optimistic about graduation.

I was advised I was not going to graduate. I felt so embarrassed not graduating with my class. I thought I'm the kid who is a senior at 20 years old with a full beard. I was humiliated, humbled but with hope. I don't know how or why, but I had faith in something. Something in my spirit said it wasn't over, it doesn't end here

It was summer time again and it was club soccer game day. I was sitting in a chair eating cereal and watching cartoons. This was my routine for years. I had a flashback. When I was approximately 11 years old, I was doing the same thing. Sitting in this chair, eating cereal and watching cartoons. Prior to game time. I finished my cereal and attempted to get up and clean my bowl. I couldn't move. I had never experienced anything like that. I yelled for my Grandmother. She came over and asked what was wrong. I told her I couldn't get up. I could hear the fear in her voice as it shook when she spoke. She said try to stand up. She yelled "get up Geno!" I still couldn't stand up. We were both shook now. She said it may be growing pains and your body is adjusting. She said just sit there and we'll reassess in 30 minutes.

Granny was right on, Thirty minutes later I stood right up. At that moment someone knocked on the door. Granny said in a kind yet stern voice, "You're not playing today!" I then advised my boys I couldn't play that day. God said. "Nope, not today son!" I had no further issues after that.

CHAPTER 14

MEXICO

The Menlo Park Mexican League selected their best players to play in a tournament in Mexico. They asked me if I could play. I asked my Granny and Coach Bebo. They both agreed I was in good hands with the folks I would be going with.

And we were off. On our way to Sonora Mexico. I was a kid from Southside Chicago with no clue about Mexico. All I wanted to do was score some goals.

Personally, I felt it was a long trip there, but I wasn't bored or irritated at the least. After all, I had a sweet Walkman and the Gucci Crew keeping me company.

By the age of 16 or so I was done with imaginary friends. At least I thought I was. While we were driving in the middle of nowhere. I imagined one of my best friends running alongside our vehicle. Kind of like Superman when he was in high school running next to the train. I imagined him periodically passing us then eventually slowing down for us. He would build up so much speed he would practically be flying. He was our protector, our guardian angel. Needless to say, I wasn't bored.

It was dark out and we were close to our Hotel. We stopped at a taco stand. The Carne Asada smelled so good. They were the best tasting tacos ever. It could have been the fact that we were super hungry. We finally arrived at the hotel. We took showers and crashed for the evening.

The next thing I heard was, "Wake up, it's time for breakfast". "Be careful there's a tiger outside." I opened my eyes and picked up my head. All of a sudden I wasn't hungry anymore. But I was super curious of course.

I got dressed and a couple of us took a look outside. We saw a literal Tiger chained to a palm tree. The Tiger was big but looked a bit unhealthy and weak. I felt sorry for her. As we walked to breakfast I didn't get near her. She was weak and looked meek. The fact is, it was a full grown Tiger and I had and displayed the utmost respect for her.

Our game wasn't until the evening. So we were told that after breakfast we were going downtown in order to walk around and stay active. I was having such a great time.

Everything was so new and adventurous.

We ate an awesome breakfast then headed downtown. Once we arrived and exited the vehicles, I looked around and actually loved what I saw. It reminded me of the old school Hawaii five-O tv show. It was 1989 and everything looked like it was 1959.

We began walking and eventually stopped at a crosswalk. I couldn't help but notice the Federales standing on almost every street corner with their machine guns in hand. I already felt small, and at that moment I felt even smaller. They were in complete control. I did feel a bit of comfort when I saw our Coach talking to one of the officers like they were old pals.

As we stood at the cross walk I felt something or someone touch the back of my arm. I turned around and there stood a random kid. The boy looked rough, dirty and had tattered clothes on. The boy reached toward me as if to touch my arm again. I didn't know what to do. Back home I would have pushed him away or punched him in the face. I was in his world. Where they spoke another language, had different customs and beliefs. And big officers with big machine guns. For that moment I felt that I was at that aggressive little fellow's mercy.

Thank God one of my fellow players yelled something in Spanish to the kid. The officer that was talking to my coach heard the commotion and walked over to us. Which was exactly what I wanted to avoid from the moment I saw the Federales. The Officer said something to the kid in an aggressive tone. The Officer then slapped the kid on the side of his head. The kid then took off running down the street. Never to be seen again. I thought I was in a movie.

I was so relieved the kid ran off. I didn't want any trouble or any extra attention focused in my direction. I was there to score goals, not get myself or anyone else in trouble. The fact that I didn't get shot up like my conscience told me I would, was a plus. Which made the adventure I was having super cool.

It was game time and it was raining like we were in the rainforest. Visibility on the field was poor. I could barely see the goalkeeper from the middle circle. The pitch was super thick with random missing patches of grass which created puddles. I was impressed with the fans. The stands were full and they were quite vociferous. Once again, it felt like I was in a movie and the curtain was about to be drawn. It was cold and kind of miserable. I loved it. The reality was it was them against us. The field was poor for both teams, no excuses. As long as there was no lightning the show must and did go on.

The match began and the crowd went wild, true story. Right off the bat I noticed the other team played well and quite professional. They were strong but fair. No ridiculous tackles or unnecessary fouls. It was about 30 minutes into the match and the rain began to come down fiercely. There was a moment or two that I could barely see more than 5 feet in front of myself. As I ran and received the ball, I could vaguely hear the crowd chanting, "Negro!

"Pinchi negro!" I then realized every time I touched the ball or got next to their side of the field they called me the "N" word and other nasty words.

As I ran back and forth I was wondering if they knew I was just a kid? Just then as I was running past the rowdy fans, something hit me on my forehead. I immediately thought, now they're throwing stuff at me. I didn't get scared, I got mad! I could barely see due to the rain but I wanted to find what they hit me with. I looked on the ground for no more than 30 seconds and noticed a huge beetle struggling in the mud.

Could it have been that giant bug that busted me on my forehead? Whatever it was that hit me, it hit me hard. I had a bit of mental relief thinking maybe it wasn't the crowd. Now I had to get revenge on that giant beetle! So I stepped on the bug. I didn't just step on it. It disappeared into the earth. Take that sucka!

Just before halftime, bam! Something hit me on the side of the head. I said there is no way that was a bug. The crowd has to be throwing stuff. The rain had dissipated to a drizzle in the wind so I could see much better. I looked on the ground and there it was! The notorious beetle was struggling in the mud again. It was personal now. I stepped on that bug for like 2 minutes. The halftime whistle blew while I was decimating my mortal enemy. My teammate Rudy Corral walked over and said, "What's going on Bobbie? "You ok over there?" In my fury I spouted out a few choice words as I explained what had occurred. Rudy laughed which then made me laugh at myself. Thank God for Rudy! He was most definitely one of my futbol heroes. By the way, the bug didn't die, true story.

Second half started, the score was 0-0 and I was motivated. It was like God was in that bug. It motivated me and woke me up out of my negative mindset. Rudy helped as well, he always did. We kicked off and the rain had basically stopped. We all could hear the Negro chant clearly now. "Negro!" "Pinchi Negro!" Blah blah blah was all I heard. I thought, I got something for you guys.

I was playing well and doing tricks with the ball. I could hear the crowd changing their tone and word usage. They wanted a show, I was going to give them a show. The ball came to me up front. I faked a shot and dribbled past the last defender. The keeper came out towards me. I did the same move. I faked a shot, he dove on the ground. I then passed the ball into the back of the net. GOAL! The crowd then chanted, Negro, Negro, Negro. Not the best word in the world to be called but it sounded a bit different. Approximately 10 minutes later I scored a second goal. The crowd went wild chanting Bovi, Bovi, Bovi! They were chanting my name now. It was a beautiful experience and I was grateful to be a part of it. I grew up a little that night. I learned alot about myself and others.

Today I watch soccer and see a whole lot of cruelty and racism toward players. My words of wisdom is this. My friends, try your best to understand that these people are ignorant. In reality they didn't make themselves racist, they were taught and learned how to be racist.

Do some research on the topic and be brave. To the people who don't like others for the color of their skin. Please do some research and be brave. You may learn something about yourselves and your lineage. And to both groups. It's called a 'game' for a reason. Do some research, and be brave.

We won the match and were hero's for an evening. Now it was time to celebrate. By the way, did I mention I had a half blond Jerry Curl? I thought of it because I remember forgetting my Jerry Curl juice at home. In the rain I was a Jerry Curl King. When it dried up my lid was dry and super frizzy. I looked like a half blonde Buckwheat! For you youngsters, Google Soul Glow. Then Google Eddie Murphy, Buckwheat's greatest hits.

We were headed to a restaurant named Los Arcos. I was also advised that Don King and Julio Cesar Chavez were going to be present at the restaurant as well. Chavez was going to fight Meldrick Taylor on March 17, 1990. We were approximately five tables away from Mr. King and Mr. Chavez. It was a fantastic night. I tried clams on a half shell with lime and hot sauce. I even tried alligator. It tasted like chicken gristle. It was good I suppose. I was offered frog legs, but I declined.

I noticed Don King looking over at me periodically. Considering we were the only melanated individuals in the place I understood. When we were about done with dinner, a few of the players told me to go get Don Kings autograph. I was shy and embarrassed but found the courage and did it. Don King said I saw you over there. What are you doing all the way over here in Mexico? I told him I was playing soccer. He laughed and said good for you. I laughed as well.

We arrived back at the hotel. I was high on adrenaline, but it wore out at the hotel. We took showers and crashed out. The air there was really moist. You take a shower and 5 minutes later, you need another.

The following morning I woke up with an upset stomach. I was in the restroom all morning. After I came out of the restroom I felt much better. I was advised to not drink the water. So of course I didn't. Then I thought back and remembered the ice cubes in the many drinks I've had throughout my trip. The Ice cubes were like the devil. Cool and refreshing until you wake up in the morning with cooties in your belly!

When we drove to our second match I saw a couple of things that I'll never forget. The first was a man walking on the sidewalk. The man was bent over and literally walking with his hands and feet. It appeared he couldn't straighten himself upright. I felt so bad for him. It tore me up and I couldn't stop thinking about him.

The second visual was a small child no more than 5 years old on a piece of cardboard. The cardboard was on the dirt ground just outside of what appeared to be a primitive bus station. I didn't understand it. Why was the baby laying there with no one to take care of him? Why was this baby so exhausted that he could sleep on that surface? And the elements surrounding him didn't faze him one bit. People passed by him as if he wasn't there. I know there's more to the story, but at the time I felt no one cared for him.

Our match began and I felt I played conservative but well. My performance was no comparison to my prior performance. It was super humid and hot. I was a bit dehydrated and it showed in my performance. I was simply grateful to survive that heat. The trip was a beautiful experience. I saw and experienced such an assortment of situations. It almost felt like this trip was a part of my youthful calling on this planet. Thank you God and all of my friends for taking such great care of me. It truly was a blessing.

School started and I was serving my time as a 2 time senior. It was embarrassing but no one ever questioned me or brought it up. With it being my second senior year of high school I was, you guessed it, ineligible. No soccer for me. I had no one to blame but myself. On the bright side. I did get a girlfriend. It was shiny and bright, until the sun went down. I'm gonna make this quick and straight. Her name was Tisha. She was absolutely stunning. Not only my opinion. But also the opinions of my so-called friends.

CHAPTER 15

GIRLFRIEND OR GIRL-FRIEND

Tisha loved my body and my lips. When we were alone she was all over me. I thought the world of her. I did notice that every once in a while when we were holding hands in the school hallway. She would randomly and abruptly release my hand. I mentally made excuses for her. After a while I got used to it and expected it. I realize now that I was the fake person, not her.

A couple of my friends at school often asked me questions about Tisha. I saw no problem with that. After all, she was super gorgeous and we simply discussed her hotness. I was oblivious to the fact that she was the only thing those two fellas and I had in common.

One day Tisha showed up at my apartment. Granny was like, "Nope!" So we hung out at the park. Tisha would even show up to my soccer practice. It made me happy and cared for. My family never showed up to my games let alone a simple practice session.

One day at school, a kid named Chris approached me in the hallway between classes. I knew Chris was trouble. He was always fighting and getting expelled from schools. A few days prior he fought a good friend of mine. So I assumed that was the reason he approached me.

Chris walked in front of me and began belittling me. I stopped walking and removed my backpack and my sweatshirt. By the way it was over 100 degrees outside. I was cool like that. I asked him are we fighting? He didn't answer my question and proceeded to belittle me again. I proceeded to put my sweatshirt and backpack once again. I then walked to my next class.

When class was over I headed toward my next class and there he was. Chris and a friend standing in the middle of the pod ready to fight. I then took off my sweatshirt and back once again. Then walked over to where Chris was standing. I believe he attempted to swing and missed. I took him down with a crash. I remember the watchers responding when Chris hit the ground. I was on top of Chris with his head between my knees. I proceed to ground and pound.

After about 4 or 5 strikes to his hands and arms which were covering his head. Someone large picked me up from behind. The person placed me on my feet and said "Bobbie, let's go to the bus!" It was Johnny breaking me out of my Ralphy trance and saving me in the process. I had guardian angels all over the place, I just didn't understand it at the time.

When I arrived at the bus school stop I saw Tisha waiting for me. Just then Chris showed up and wanted revenge. I told him "I'm not fighting you." He attempted to verbally provoke me to fight. I got a vibe that Tisha wanted me to fight as well. I stuck to my word and told him again, "I'm not fighting you." Tisha and I got on the bus and noticed Chris following the bus in a car. I explained to her what happened earlier. She asked if I was going to fight him, I responded, "No."

Once we arrived at the bus drop off point at the park, Tisha and I exited the bus. Chris exited his vehicle and was ready to fight. Once again I told him I wasn't fighting him. Chris and Tisha both looked at me dumbfounded. Chris began belittling me in front of Tisha. I didn't care, I wasn't going to fight.

That was the last time Tisha and I hung out. Chris was expelled due to his priors. Years later I was told some rumors about Tisha. Truth or fiction Tisha wasn't a bad person. And I pray that her life flowed in the direction she chose. May God bless you all!

CHAPTER 16

PROM NIGHT

My second senior year I was asked to go to the school prom by Melissa Bermudez. We were good friends and I was honored to attend with her. The only issue I had was money. She reassured me that money will not be a problem, and she advised me to not worry about money. She was a beautiful blessing without a doubt.

Prom night I dressed up in my Tux and took pictures with my mom and Granny. My mother was living with us at the time. It was short lived due to her addictive nature. Melissa picked me up in the current model Mustang 5.0. It was white and looking super fly. I think that was even before Vanilla

Ice hit the scene. I thought, "Maybe she really likes me?" I was oblivious to that sort of stuff.

We danced the night away and had a great time. As the night progressed I thought more and more about us not dating in the past. Well I thought the night was young and at the moment we were headed in the right direction.

We left the prom a little early and went to an after party. I had no license to drive. I had only driven approximately 2 times in my life. Melissa wanted me to drive so I was like heck yeah! I drove and we didn't die. I know Melissa was nervous in that passenger seat though.

Once we arrived at the after party we had a few drinks. Melissa pulled me aside and presented me with a bracelet. It was a super thick gold bracelet. It had to have been expensive. I gave her a big kiss and thought, yup that's my girl for sure. I went to the restroom and grabbed another drink. When I returned to the spot we were hanging out at, Melissa was nowhere to be found. Approximately 30 to 45 minutes later Melissa walked from the hallway of the home with a guy in tow. She then asked me if I wanted to stay or if I was ready to go. I felt there was no reason to be there so I told her I was ready to leave. Melissa proceeded to find me a ride home and that was that. No hard feelings, we were just friends right?

CHAPTER 17

GOOD THOUGHTS ONLY

One day when I returned home from soccer practice. I opened the door and walked in. I turned around and looked up. As my vision slowly adjusted from light to dark I saw 2 figures sitting at the kitchen table. I stared for a second at the unfamiliar face. My head tilted to one side like a Panther visualizing a potential target.

It was the local drug dealer sitting at our kitchen table with my grandmother. My flesh said attack immediately, but my spirit said breathe. Mr. Drug dealer said, “Hello young man.” I grit my teeth and said, “What's up?” I then headed straight to my room. I sat in my room and reminded myself that Granny could take care of herself. She had a past that I knew nothing of. I could hear them talking and it appeared his visit was a cry for help and free therapy.

In the past I remember my mom looking all strung out with that guy. I had no love for him. His very presence tainted our sacred sanctuary. I remember myself wanting him to get out of our apartment immediately. Approximately two Months later I was watching the local news. It was a drug deal gone bad. One dead with no suspects. When they showed the victim’s name and photo (on the television) I said to myself, it was him. It was the drug dealer that was in my home. I heard and felt my heart beating in my chest. My knees literally got shaky and weak. I felt like Peter Parker allowing the criminal to run past him. I realized that the scenario and situation was different. But I was thinking negatively about that man and the next thing I heard about him was that he was murdered. Please be mindful of your thoughts.

We were headed to a club soccer tournament in Phoenix. My best friend Jose Miranda said play well because college scouts are going to be watching you. When he told me that bit of information it motivated me because someone cared. I honestly didn't think that if I played well they would give me a soccer scholarship. School and I didn't really get along. I thought if the US Olympic Development folks couldn't get me in, how then could a College?

I played like a Champion in that tournament. We were told that some of Arizona's best players would be in that tournament. With no arrogance, it didn't matter to me. It never mattered who I played against. I controlled this vessel and I had full trust that it could and would do whatever I requested of it.

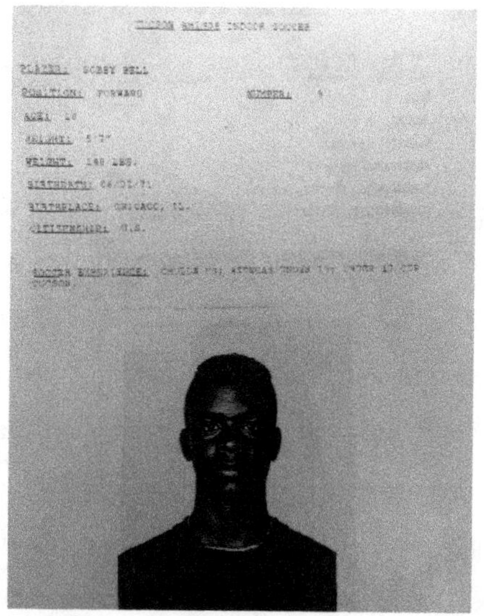

[illegible]

PLAYER: BOBBY BELL

POSITION: FORWARD NUMBER: [illegible]

AGE: [illegible]

HEIGHT: [illegible]

WEIGHT: 148 LBS.

BIRTHDATE: [illegible]

BIRTHPLACE: CHICAGO, IL.

CITIZENSHIP: U.S.

SOCCER EXPERIENCE: [illegible]

I scored goals, got assists, did backflips and flip throws. I'll explain my flip throw knowledge shortly. I was fouled hard and never retaliated. The one time I attempted to retaliate was when I crushed a player's ego and he responded by calling me the "N' word. I went after the player but was stopped by Jose and another player from the opposing team. Kobe Washington asked me what happened. I told him and he then went at his own teammate. I was dumbfounded at the time. After the game we all talked and Kobe explained he was recruited to the same College. Which was Yavapai College.

Now let me give you my flip throw history. A flip throw is essentially a front handspring in which the player flips forward by putting the ball on the ground while holding it with both hands. Then flipping forward and throwing it on the field. Roy Almazan taught me the flip throw in 1983 when we were in Jr. High School. Roy said one of his family members taught him the flip throw. It was now time to put the flip throw on the map and into the mainstream. In the end, the Yavapai coach and player scouts were impressed with my performance.

High School graduation was days away and I honestly wasn't sure I was going to make it, again. I remember going classroom to classroom to ask my teachers for my final grades.

Melissa pushed me to do this to determine if I needed to purchase a cap and gown. The final teacher gave me a hard time but finally said you're graduating.

Soon after I graduated I was notified by the YC head coach Mike Pantalione that they wanted to offer me a soccer scholarship to YC. I was honored to be given a scholarship to play futbol with some super skilled ball players. Pima College also offered me a scholarship. I was truly honored. I wasn't going to YC all by myself. Jose of course and my good friend Justin Ground was going as well. Justin's dad drove us up to YC for our recruiting trip. It was a great time until my ego got the best of me. I tried chewing tobacco for the first time. I got sick and couldn't go to the house party. God said, not today!

CHAPTER 18

COLLEGE

Coach Bebo drove Jose and I to the YC dorms. On the trip there my gear was in the trunk, and Jose's stuff was mostly on the roof. Halfway there one of the suitcases on the roof popped open. Jose's clothes were all over the freeway. We all got out of the vehicle and began running in circles all over the freeway like we were in a comedy show. It all worked out thank God.

Jose was my roommate all throughout College. We had bunk beds at YC. I was on the top bunk. Marvin Cassler and Jose Corona were on the other side of the wall.

The Yavapai College soccer team was in its second year when we arrived. Their first year they were undefeated. They couldn't compete for the

National Championship due to the NJCAA rules of being a first year program. We still had half of the players from last year and some new quality talent.

By the end of the season we were the first team to ever win a National Championship at Yavapai College with a record of 21-01-01. My second year at Yavapai we lost our first game of the season in the National Championship final. Our record was 21-01-00.

A few memorable moments for me at YC were I had a girlfriend throughout College. Her name was Diane. She was one of the smartest people in the school. She was beautiful and a basketball player. Yes, she was taller than me. After our 2 years at YC we went to different schools. The following year at our alumni soccer match I was informed by a friend of Diane's that she was pregnant. It shocked me to the core. I didn't know if I should scream, pass out or both. But that's a part of life. Diane and I had a great time at YC and I love her for it.

Another memorable moment at YC occurred when we were driving to a party. Peter, who was a fellow teammate, was driving his girlfriend, Jose and I to a party. We had to drive through some hills to get to the party. Jose and I were in the back seat. Jose was talking to his girlfriend and Peter started speeding up a little. Someone mentioned that he was going a bit fast and the next thing I saw was a wall in front of us, then complete silence. It felt like we were floating in a spaceship. Then Bam and reality kicked back in and I realized we were sliding on the roof of the car. Jose and I were basically surfing on the roof while Peter and his girlfriend were hanging upside down in their seatbelts. Jose and I looked at each other and he said there's blood on your shirt.

Physically I was the only one to get hurt. When we flipped the silence was us flying and the bam is when my face hit the roof. My teeth went through my bottom lip. I was taken to the ER and they stitched me up. When I came out from getting stitches it seemed like half the school was in the lobby crying and thinking we were dead. I love you guys.

The final memorable moment was putting the flip throw on the map. You heard it right! I did the flip throw heard all around the Country. I was the first player in history to perform the flip throw in 2 National Championships and winning one. So now you know my friends. I didn't create it, but I put it on the map in the United States.

Mike Pantilione finally retired after an unreal career. Our 1990 YC team has since been inducted into the YC Hall of Fame. Today YC's overall record is 636-63-30. Mike Pantilione was one of the best all-around coaches ever. No matter what sport or level. The numbers don't lie.

The head coach of the Springfield, Illinois Prairie Stars visited YC to recruit soccer players. Aydin Gonulsen was the head coach of Sangamon

State University and he announced to us that he wanted us all. He said he wanted as many of us as he could get to win a National Championship. We all had multiple offers from various colleges. I chose Springfield because it made sense somehow. Maybe because it was close to Chicago and I felt had something to prove. Thank God Jose, Tony, Marvin and Jose chose Sangamon State as well. I was so happy we were all going together.

When we arrived in Springfield we were assigned host families. They were like our Guardian Angels. If we were in need of anything within regulations of course. They tried their best to assist us. Jose and I had the same host family. It made sense, we were always together. The great and wonderful Christofilakos family blessed us with their friendship and kindness. The Gonulsen and Christofilakos families were a blessing to us Arizona boys.

Everyone was super loving, but we spent most of our time with these two families. After meeting these two families I knew we made the correct decision to attend SSU.

We had players from Arizona, St Louis, Africa, Illinois, Mexico, France, Kansas, and of course Turkey. If I left any State or Country out please forgive me boys. You know I love you. My first year at SSU we had a solid team. With such an assortment of players, it worked out nicely. We lost in the NAIA National Championship semi-finals.

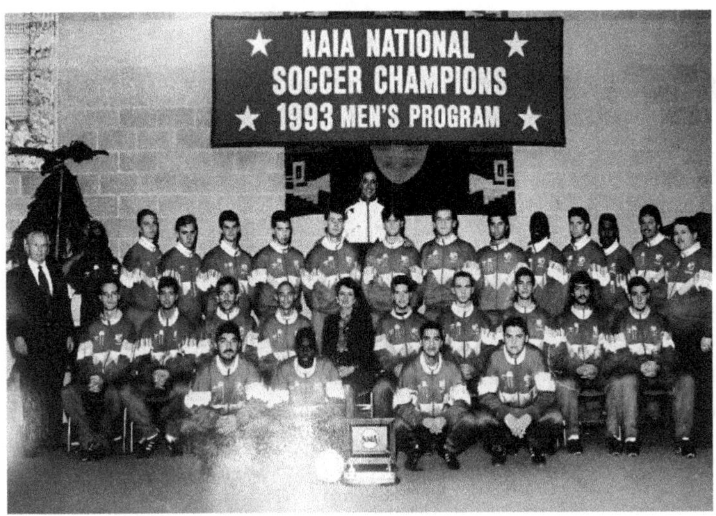

The next day I vividly remember watching the National Championship finals with my teammates from the stands. I closed my eyes and breathed in the chilled air. I listened to the crowd cheer for the contestants. I watched the warriors out on the pitch battle for what could have been ours. We didn't deserve the trophy because we didn't do what was necessary to obtain it.

I wanted to absorb as much as I could in order to use it for next season's preparation. When the match was over and the crowd cheered for the new National Champs. I remember them playing Queen, we are the champions. I fought hard not to break out in tears. Not because I was sad. But because I wanted what was supposed to be mine. Even as I write this, I had to take a breather because the tears won't allow me to see. Aydin Gonulsen was a genius.

The following summer I was informed by the SSU counselors that I was short a few credit hours. I was advised to take summer school in Tucson if I wanted to be eligible. I thought here we go again. I wasn't the same person I was 3 years ago. And I wasn't going to let this happen again. I completed the classes and passed them all with a C or better.

Then I was advised I had to take 2 classes at SSU if I wanted to be eligible. The courses were considered summer school and were to be taken before the season started. I didn't fight it and made it happen. I took the classes and passed them with a C or better. I was proud of myself. I was a changed kid. Passing multiple college courses in the summer. When no more than 3 years ago I couldn't pass high school classes.

Our second season at SSU had begun. Tony and Marvin moved on and Joseph and Luis came in from Yavapai who won another National Championship. What a blessing they were.

Game day was close and us Yavi-boys were stoked. We knew what we were capable of and were ready to put our talents on display. We even had cheerleaders. Not officially but they were, as Hammer would say, 2 legit. Then DeJa Vu slapped me in the face with its strong hand.

I was informed that I was ineligible to play. I couldn't believe it. I thought, did I miss one of the classes they advised me to take? What did I do wrong? I immediately felt like I let my boys down. My heart was broken. This time I did what was called of me and it still wasn't enough.

I was told to suit up because they weren't sure what was going on. Just before our first official game I was given a green light. Coach sat me on the bench to start. Micky Tennant started on the right side which was where I played. Micky played well and showed his strengths. The game was close.

I believe I came in at the half. Jose whispered that I could beat the guys on my side and he's going to send the ball. As soon as the half started, I immediately noticed my opponent wasn't respecting me by giving me so much space. So I kept it slow for a couple runs up and down the field. Jose received the ball and I knew exactly what he was going to do. Something we've done since we were 8 years old and perfected at Yavapai. Without looking he turned and hit the ball from the left side to the opposite corner flag.

The defender that was watching me was nowhere to be found. Just that fast it was the keeper and I. Goal! I believe that may have been my first touch on the ball. The shot wasn't pretty, but it went into their net. Shortly after that goal, I scored another. I really wanted my spot back.

I was a senior and this was my final college playing experience. I played with players that had so much God given talent. Players with beautiful yet tough hearts. Young men that had natural athleticism and shaped all their focus and skills around that soccer ball. The same as I had. You were all a blessing from God.

At one point in the season us players weren't getting along. Go figure with all the testosterone and machismo on the team. Nothing physical but there was a whole lot of bickering and gossiping. Somehow coach Aydin heard about the nonsense we were creating. The next practice session after the coach's discovery. He told us we weren't touching the ball. We were getting into groups of 4 to 5 players and having a sit down. We were not to get up until the group sorted out what they needed to. By the end of practice everybody was hugging and chanting like we were in New Orleans drinking beer through a street cone. By the way, that truly happened. Aydin Gonulsen was a genius.

We are now in the National Championship tournament. We beat everyone and are now in the National Championship final. A day before the final. Jose and Jose asked all of the players if they wanted to go to Church. They did the same thing at Yavapai and we won the match. I believe praying is like meditation. You calm and realign your spirit. It was our honest prayer to God that put our minds in the right place. I prayed that no one from either team gets hurt. I prayed for strength and courage to achieve something thought impossible. I prayed to conquer my fear of the unknown.

Let me tell you a story of the genius that is Aydin Gonulsen. Jose, Jose and I drove to the field with Aydin on game day. At one point Aydin says with total surprise, "We are going to win!" "I can see it." "I just had a vision! I had a vision and we are going to win."

Was he just playing us in order to put our minds in the proper place? Or did the Holy Spirit give him a vision of what's to come? Personally I believed him. At that moment Aydin taught me to always think positive thoughts. When it gets difficult, don't dwell on those thoughts and that state of mind. Believe God is there for you. You have to truly believe like we did at the tournament. Let go with complete and total faith.

I'm not ending this short story of my life with our Championship win. The win is actually on YouTube. It looks real close to black and white. It's beautiful nonetheless. I'm going to tell you a short story about fear and strength.

It was 1992, my first year at Sangamon State. We were playing an away game. The match started and all was normal and well. Then I heard voices that sounded like soldiers. And stomping that sounded like boots on the ground. I'm sure it was in my head but it felt like the ground was shaking. The ball went out of bounds and as I looked up and off to a distance. I saw a football team all geared up marching toward the field. Once again, I thought I was in a movie. I looked at Johnny 'O' and said help with my eyes. Johnny 'O' was a certified beast. More like a kind giant that you don't want to upset. I looked around and our entire team was stopped in their tracks looking at the football team. I'm sure everyone was thinking, "What are you going to do to us?"

The football team marched around the field circling ¾ of the field. They stopped and stood there on the chalk line. You can probably guess what I said. Yup, I said, "I got something for you boys." The match was a formidable one. They played us tough. But the trick up my sleeve was that God prepared me for this moment in Mexico. And I wanted the ball.

As an athlete you know when you're feeling it. It's like your 3rd eye opens and you become super focused. You feel that there is no one that can stop you. I yelled for the ball when I saw a small opening.

Ian, who eventually became the head coach of the Belize National team had the ball. I was just inside the circle just outside their 18 yard line. Ian was a baller, but was having a frustrating game. You could see it on his face and in his voice. I yelled again, "Pass me the ball Ian.

It was slow motion in my head. Ian smashed the ball toward me with a low drive. I could see him cussing me out as he struck the ball. There was a player just behind me literally with hands on. I controlled the drive with my right foot which popped the ball up just to my right side about knee high. I turned to my right then, bam! I hit the ball with my left foot.

The ball hit the keeper's left goal post, went behind him then hit the right goal post. The keeper didn't move.

I ran toward Johnny 'O' and he picked me up like I was a 2 year old on top of the world. While I was on top of the world, I saw the football players' faces. Some had their mouths open, some were clapping and other were staring at Johnny and me with disgruntled faces.

I immediately bent my body downward so Johnny could put me down. Johnny said stay up Bobbie. I didn't want to though.

I did what I came to do. I fought my fear and showed the enemy we're not the bad guys. And I was not rubbing it in their faces shows them that I acknowledge they weren't the enemy either. We were simply on different futbol teams.

Aydin O. Gonulsen passed on July 6, 2021. My teammates Patrick Chae, James Hemmingway, and Ron Sanlin passed on as well. We were all inducted into the SSU Hall of Fame. We are the last team in history to win a futbol National Championship for SSU. This is because the school name changed to the University of IllInois in Springfield. Yavapai inducted us into the Yavapai College Hall of Fame as well. We will be remembered as the first team to ever win a futbol National Championship there.

My friends, love is the answer. God is love. Therefore the answer is God.

ABOUT THE AUTHOR

Bobbie Bell is a true man of God. He has played soccer most of his life. He has won championships in college, and played professional soccer. Bobbie Bell worked for the department of corrections and retired after 20 years of service. He obtained a personal trainer and nutrition certification. He is now learning about the spirit from the best teacher possible. The highest God. With assistance from his human angels on earth. Bobbie is now on a journey to obtain true freedom and to heal. His goal is to heal as many beautiful souls as possible. In the process maintaining his physical and spiritual fitness. A quote from the great Bob Marley, "Emancipate yourself from mental slavery, none but ourselves can free our mind." Some say

Bobbie is homeless, he says he's on a journey to discover what true freedom is. Also to learn from the Holy Spirit, nature, and the Supreme Being known as God.

Printed in the USA
CPSIA information can be obtained
at www.ICGtesting.com
LVHW020852051223
765518LV00075B/2004